THE
PROCESS
CODE

The Process Code

Unlocking your past to live your future
Josh Carmichael

*"When you forgive, you in no way change the past—
but you sure do change the future."*
~ Bernard Meltzer

<u>*Do you know what brought you to where you
are now?*</u>
*To all of you who want more out of life.
More money, more passion, more love, more
excitement, and better health.
This is for you.*

11/14/19

To a man who
is the closest thing
to a brother or twin.
We have more in common
than I previously
knew.
It's great getting to
know you more
and watching you
go after your career.
You're incredible
and truly gifted.
Remember that.

Much love
Brother
Always

Introduction

"The beginning is where we all start."

In this book, you will find keys to unlock the tools that will provide you a plethora of exploration. Through the pages you will turn not only turn pages but will evolve and grow into the YOU, you were meant to BE. Self is something we all forget and have left so much of ourselves in the past that we have disconnected from the very essence of who we are. IE: How many times have you heard that VOICE in the back of your mind telling you to go for it, try something new, or to just take a shot. Ask a person out, ask for that promotion, confront your teacher about your grades, ask your parents for the car, jump off the diving board, live to your greatest potential? Well, perhaps you are not ready for the last one, but you have heard the voice, correct?

The **Process CODE** will show you the way. A complete guide into a world of hopes, dreams, and reality. By taking the steps to unlock the past and be BOLD enough to stand in front of the new you and face the truth! By doing so, you will feel more, experience more and be more successful in the things you set out to achieve. If you are ready for that, then you are READY to begin.
Welcome to **The Process CODE**

Code definition:

To convert (the words of a message) into a particular code to convey a secret meaning.

~ Josh Carmichael

The Process CODE

Will teach you and give you the tools to unlock your past, dis-cover why you are in the place you are now and reveal your true passion and how to live for your future. Based on three things that may be the cause of our pain. If you were Bullied, Beaten or Abused, you will get a lot from this course.

Bullied; Includes, shoving, name-calling, being picked on, spit on, locker slammed, tripped, knocked down, or punched.

Beaten; slapped, punched, kicked, whipped, tortured.

Abused; Neglected, starved, locked up, locked in, verbally, emotionally or sexually abused.

Do any of these connect to you? I can relate to all three.

Stress

What causes it? Why do we stress about things we cannot see? I believe you will begin to see why you may stress over things you do not understand or project in your mind, or thoughts that cause the paranoia and fear, which causes the lack of, or missing from the type of stress. "I'm not good enough." This is a self-esteem issue. We will cover it. "Those people hate me." That's speculation and false information. You have no idea what others think or feel about you unless they express it. We will cover this too. "If I don't pay the electric bill they will shut off my power." That may be true, but I'm betting if you call them and explain the situation, you'll realize there are a few options and you may be able to get an extension. now, instead of putting energy into the overdue bill, focus on what you want in life. The money will come to you a lot faster when you are focused on the good and the progressive vibration. We will get you to a better place during this. Just dive in and enjoy the challenges and please commit to the work.

Looking for the Solution

I f you are like me, you avoid finishing self-help books that you have started, because of some deep-seated, or unconscious fear of actually changing the patterns that keep us from achieving our goals and dreams. Is this you? If so, then welcome to the majority. Many of us pick up self-help books in a time of need, or when we are looking for the solution to an existing problem. The truth is, *they never work!* Right? We buy one after another and sometimes display them on our bookshelves (especially the popular, or best selling ones) to show our guests, or passers-by how smart, evolved and/or enlightened we are. That WE cared enough to fix ourselves and buy the trendy books that shape lives and change the way we think, act and work.

But, it's not true, is it? Let's be honest with ourselves for a moment. We not only spend endless amounts of money

on books we never finish we also never do the work!
How many of you own up to this right now? Raise your
hand and say "yes!"

Ah Ha! I thought so! I said it too I was so proud
of myself one summer I read 75 books. Yes, in less than
three months I had read 75+ self-help and self-realization
books that I could now proudly display on my bookshelf
and mantel for everyone to see. Sad thing was, "I couldn't
remember what any of them said." So, much like you, I realized I was not looking for a "self-help" book, I was looking
for THE SOLUTION.

The Solution to all my questions, fears and doubts.
Because, I began to see a pattern that I would purchase books
when I was feeling depressed, or was alone, felt lonely.

So, each week, or month I would get more and more
and more... This went on for nearly 20 years. Then one

day, while packing to move, I realized not only how heavy all the books were when packed into four large boxes, but that I no longer needed them because none of them worked. Not one of these self-help books changed my life into what I wanted to be. Not one! And I was ANGRY!

I was angry that I had read all these books gained some useful terms and perhaps I gained some knowledge, but it was only good when telling others how to fix their lives, while my life seemed to remain in constant struggle and flux.

So, join me now on a NEW attempt of figuring out THE SOLUTION. I promise you, after all the research I have done and 100's of partially read self-help books, this is the BEST thing that works.

With Great Passion and Love
~ Josh Carmichael

Contents

WARNING: This book will change your life. Before you jump in be sure you are ready for change and growth. It will make you question things you have perhaps overlooked and brought you to a higher frequency or vibration that will begin to attract a greater life and lifestyle.

Are you ready?

ACKNOWLEDGMENT

There are so many amazing and gifted people who have affected and/or touched my life through the years. Harry Mastrogeorge, Janet Alhanti, Eric Morris, Denis Johnson, Kahlil Gibran, David Deida, Dan Millman and "The Way of the peaceful warrior" were one of the first. Louise Haye, whom I had the chance to work with very early on, Joseph Campbell, Robert Bly whose writings still inspire. I'm grateful to all the teachers who challenged me and the US NAVY for making me a man. A special thank you to my two sons who inspire me by just being who they are and to the woman who has filled my heart and given me the balance I so longed for, thank you, Nancy, you are a gift and a blessing.

Wait! Grab a pen or pencil, a note pad for extra thoughts and be ready to jump in. Ready? Shall we begin?

1 If you are like me

If you are like me,
you know how many times it may take to get things right.
Right? Or, the journey may take a while to reach the
destination that makes you stop and say "eureka!" I have
found it! If you are like me, you will continue this journey
and search for a better you and a better understanding of
yourself and those around you. If you are like me, you'll do
the work needed to tap into your past and realize your future.
If you are like me, you know there's a power inside of you
that is crying to get out. Perhaps, the books before this, or
the studies in the past were inspirational and moving, but
forgot one crucial thing, or element. The tools! They forgot to
uncover, or teach you the tools and how to use them. We will
cover the tools in the process of this book, so stick around,
I promise you this will affect your life and not only will you
get the tools and fill your toolbox, you will then recognize
things in others and learn to coach and help others on their
journey. If you are like me, you aspire to be greater, happier,
more financially stable, healthier, live your dream job, find
love, have a family, buy a house, travel, attract great friends,
share ideas and live in the moment. If you are like me, you
want to get to the point without the redundant meanings
and overkill of poetic prose that fill the space in a book, but
is never referred to or remembered once you have finished.
If you are like me, you'll get more out of this quicker process
and begin using its teachings and revelations asap. If you are
like me, you will crave more and have a tastier desire. If you
are like me, you procrastinate and/or avoid the truth. You
are living in the memories of the past that keep repeating

themselves. You make excuses for not having what you want. You are in the same place you were five years ago. You find yourself daydreaming more than taking action. If you are like me, it's time for a change. Are you like me?

2 The Dilemma

Before we can begin the process, we must look at what's going on now and why you are here. It's called the Dilemma because there tend to be two or more alternatives or options. Sometimes these are called conflicts. It's the state of being where you may feel stuck or undecided and uncomfortable in at the moment you are in them and don't know how to get out, or what to do to change the situation. Does this sound familiar? It may be happening right now. You purchased this book, or it was given as a gift and there's a part of you that doubts already. Maybe you are doubting the book, or if the book will help. Maybe, you are doubting yourself and the fact you don't feel ready, or maybe you're afraid to let go of your past, not deal with your feelings, emotions, or other people as a result. I get it. It happens to all of us in one way or another. Just know, you are not alone. The key is, where do these dilemmas come from? Why are they part of our existence? To answer those two questions let's go backward int time for a moment to when you were younger. I know this may seem abrupt, but you are here for a reason, let's not waste time with too many words and stories based on other people. This book The Process Code is about YOU! It's a personal journey you take into yourself and your life's history to come out the other side shining brighter than before. It's tailored to you the reader with a specific goal. To affect change in your life and to uncover the patterns that have kept you where you are up to this point. Everyone will have a different answer, different story and different outcomes. But, for now, let's get back to you.

Where do these dilemmas come from? To answer that, we need to know what is the most common dilemma in your life at this time? *Note, you can use this formula over and over again until it becomes habit to challenge and work through all future situations. For now, pick one. Write it down here. Currently my dilemma is?:_____

_____

_____

_____

_____

_____

_____

_____

_____

_____

You got it? I don't even need to know what it is, because this works on each scenario. Here's an example: Let's say you wrote "I hate my job, or the job I'm doing right now and I'm not making enough money to support myself and the lifestyle I wish, but I'm afraid to quit or find other work because I am not sure how to survive in the interim". In this case, you have described your dilemma, which is based on fear. By the way, you'll find as you ask these questions on your journey that a lot of the hesitations, or issues you will face are based on fear. Again, you may not have been given the tools yet to uncover these things, but how does that feel when you acknowledge that you are afraid? Okay, afraid of what? This is where you write it out. Why does it help to write it out? The act of writing puts into motion an act of understanding and action. What are you afraid of in your current dilemma? _____

_____

_____

_____

_____

_____

_____

_____

_____

_____

Got it? Now read it aloud. How does that feel when you admit it and acknowledge it? Guess what? You just gave the fear less power and the new possibility more. Now, let's go a little further with this. The fear has had its way in and around your thoughts and/or disbeliefs for sometime now. Can you remember when, what year in life or what event happened in life when these disbeliefs began to happen? Was there trauma in life that affected you? I'm not asking you to analyze your entire life here, just a simple check in to see if at this time you can recognize when it began and perhaps what created this. ? Take a moment (Pause)… Okay, now write it down here._____

_____

_____

_____

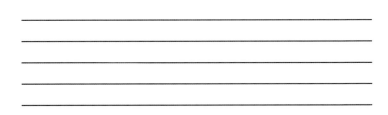

If you were successful in pinpointing the moment, then a big Yee-haw! That's progress!! If not, don't worry it will come and not all of us know or even want to know every detail in life. But, there's a formula to this that works and I will walk you through it step by step. This was the first step. Identifying the dilemma. I ask you, are you satisfied with your choice? If you are then we can move forward, if not go back now before moving to the next chapter and change your answer, because this will come up throughout **The Process Code**. Speaking of which, that's our next chapter.

3 Beyond the Ego
"Self-esteem is the key to success."

Since birth,
you have been a part of the id and ego. As we look into the similarities of these two and how they are connected to the now superego, we can learn to dis-cover some of the misunderstandings we've all most likely encountered in life. The id (according to Freud) is the instinctual drive and libido. It's the body's needs, wants, desires. The id has no conscious thought of rationalization, it only seeks pleasure and in more common terms is called "Chaos." Let's call it the dark side for the moment and understand its the confusion without guidance. Think childlike and the outbursts, or desires we all

had as children. Although you may not remember all of them, I bet your parents and grandparents or aunts and uncles or cousins could recall a few of them. They may not have known how to describe the mood swings or tantrums, but we can now. If, you look at child psychology and the growth charts and hormonal changes, etc, you can begin to see patterns as well. We are tackling the ego-self here, as this is something, in my opinion, we all fight to understand consciously or subconsciously. And, please allow me to define what I mean here about conscious and subconscious. The subconscious is where we hold the past pain, fear, anger, tragedy, and loss. The subconscious is what we will be tapping into throughout this process to unlock those patterns of avoidance. To unleash and let go of the shutdown. The conscious is the state of being now. Our goal here is to awaken that state, allow it to expand beyond your wildest dreams and live in the now, or in the conscious realm. Got it? Okay, back to the ego-self and how it takes over the id at some point in life and becomes one of two things. It plays the roles of balance between the id and the super-ego. The ego, in essence, isn't a bad thing, as we've been told, or perhaps if you are like me, called in the past. Have you ever been called egotistic? Or, told your head is too big that you have too much ego? Or, "Oh I don't want to inflate your ego any further?" Yeah, I know I have. That comes from one of two things. One, it stems from the other person jealous of your confidence, or perhaps your looks which don't define you, or your ego. Two, it comes from their lack of understanding exactly what ego is. So, what is ego and how can we go beyond it? Ego is the master of the id and super-ego. As mentioned, it creates a real balance and a sense of self-awareness. Ego, in modern times, means "Self-esteem," or the worth self. The self-worth is why you are here and the ego, as you will soon learn is the best part of the three, id, ego and super-ego. The ego, in my opinion, has been confused in terms with the super-ego, which isn't discussed much and perhaps some of you haven't even heard of it until now. Honor the ego and the worth of self and let's bring the unconscious part of that ego-self into the reality of the conscious and begin to cherish it. Narcissists or narcissism comes from the Super-ego. The super-ego has been mainly taught to us by our peers, or parents instilling or applying their guidance and influence over us. The super-ego is a perfect example of living for our parents. Because of their early influence in our lives, the patterns are formed to create, fantasize, formulate and take actions based on how they have taught us, or shown us by example. Yes, we are a product of our parents like it or not. I see the super-ego as status quo, or politically correct. The super-ego is or can be locked in confusion as well as it's affected by religion and holds unconscious guilt to it. You are welcome to further investigate, or research the terms and meanings or depth of the id, ego, and super-ego on your own. For now, we will use the ego as the master and the focus for where we want to go in this process.

"It's true that I have a healthy ego; Anybody who creates does." - Barbara Streisand

With that said, How do you get to a healthy ego and why is it so important? Getting beyond the ego, is to first tap into what may be stored inside. So, before you begin The Process Code, or the actual process within this code, we need to expand your knowledge of where that lies in you.

Some of you may be very full of yourself and perhaps eager to proceed. You might have even skipped over a few essential phrases already. Did you just read what I wrote? Okay, that was a test to see if you were still following along. Great. Even if you are full of yourself and maybe anxious about moving forward, you will find the parallels or the ego, id and super-ego that may be just the slap in the face kind of a wakeup call you need. Let's do an ego test, or as I like to call it a self esteem check in. Ready?

1. Do you worry about what other people think of you?

_____

2. How often do you think positive thoughts about yourself? Daily? Weekly? Rarely? Never?_____

3. When I talk to others, I often cannot look them in the eyes. True/False?_____

4. Are you happy with the person you are today?_____
If not, tell us why?_____

_____

_____

5. I want to improve (list one thing) about myself._____

_____

_____

_____

6. I carry guilt from my past? True/False?_____

_____

7. I'm confident in my self and self esteem. Yes/No?_____

8. How would you rate your self esteem level? Very low? Low? Average? Excellent?_____

If you chose excellent, you can put the book away, you have completed the work, we are done here. You still here?

Okay, how did you measure up? Hmmm, I'm guessing we all need improvement right? Your self-esteem isn't that secure, or you wouldn't be here to improve yourself, right? I know when I was coming up in the acting world and I threw myself to the wolves, I had no idea what I was doing and criticism hurt. It still does, but I see it as all positive now. But, I wish I would have had a structure, or book, some sort of guidance like this in my life at that time. A journey or process that wasn't about fulfilling the author's ego or self-worth by writing secret prose that explained case studies of others I couldn't relate to, or scientific theories that spun me so far back inside my head that I was getting further away from my feelings and my truth. I tried them all, I tell you. I have a plethora of superfluous knowledge in there floating around and it comes in handy when I'm questioned, but it doesn't make me live in the moment of my true self as this process does. You see, I only have my lessons to share. I've been my human experiment for 30 years. Self-discovery has been my motto and goals or passion for decades. I wasn't born into it, or even had powerful influences in my life growing up, Matter of fact, as you might know, I was a shy stuffed and low self-esteem kid, who never raised their hand in class, was put into special education at the age of six, because they thought I couldn't read. I read very well and I was an intelligent kid, I was just so introverted and shy from the abuse I endured by my peers and parents, that I was too afraid to speak up. I was afraid to be wrong, or be laughed at. I already had enough bullies after me, I didn't need more. I went through my entire school years like this. High school was a little better as I found art classes and the teachers more receptive to my more creative ideas, but they didn't know where to place me, or how to place me at that time, so I felt unheard and alone. I found it was better to talk with my animals on the ranch, then people. The nod from my dogs or the silence from other animals seemed to confirm that I could communicate quite well, it just wasn't from the right people around me. The military was the turning point. I had to stand up and be heard or get beaten not only physically but emotionally as well. At that time, I dis-covered psychol-ogy and the essence of man. I began reading about human emotions. That exploration of self has led me to reveal this process to you. By actually living it and using it, I've made notes along the way and kept adding to the process until it had enough depth to be exposed. So here you go, I give to you the tools that I feel will and can unlock anyone's past and allow you/them to reveal your passions, truths, desires, goals, careers, self-worth, self-value and self-esteem to live a better more positive life. When you are asked the right questions and you challenge yourself to take yourself more seriously, you will uncover the ego and self-esteem self that can and will stand for what you truly desire.

> *"You can never stop learning about your-self. It's never-ending."* - Josh Carmichael

Side note: We need to look at your friends right now in your life. Family is a different story and more complicated, so let's look at your friends. Who's the most successful in your group? Are they living their dream? Are they happy? What is the average annual income of your friend group? How do you feel when you are around them or share your ideas with them? Are they supportive? Do they drain you? Are you happy to see them and share them? Look around you and study the facts. Are you where you want to be? That's obvious, or you wouldn't be here. Can your current group provide the growth or stage for you to shine on? Are they truly secure and giving? I'm guessing not. Here's a wakeup call. You are only as successful as your friends. If you want to be more successful, or be around others who inspire you, you'll have to break apart of just allow the change and watch how fast your old friends disappear. It's true, I've done it several times and it is painful at times because there are those you want to help and lift up, and you see potential in them, but you cannot carry others. Never, it's not your job. So, let go of that old pattern of self that thinks you have to save the world. Hell, you haven't even saved yourself yet! Change your vibration, your energy, and your friends will change. If it's the inspiration you seek, you are welcome to join our group at any time. We hold seminars and power group weekends often. See our schedule and links at the back of this book. Or, you can always look on our website www.TheProcessCode.com. We invite you to join us and never again worry about finding the right group. I created this course because I was always outgrowing friends my age. I was 26 and I was holding a spiritual seminar in the Hollywood hills, in a small community called Beachwood Canyon. There was a park there, I had created some artwork for and had met wonderful and enlightened individuals while visiting. So, it seemed like the perfect place. As we were in the middle of a group session one night, one of the older gentlemen spoke up. He was about 15 years my senior and blankly said "How do you know so much? I mean I've been studying for many years and you know or have this knowing and understanding that's beyond your years." I simply replied with a "Why thank you. I just feel it." That was it, I was speaking my truth and I did feel it, and the awareness doesn't have an age category, and it's not afraid of dropping in anytime. I believe now looking back, I was just more open to allowing everything to come in. I never judged any of it and it flowed through me. I was grateful and blessed. But, I couldn't get enough. By that I mean, I needed more and more inspiration, so I began the learning annex and volunteered at toastmasters and went to books signings and seminars weekly. I was in three acting classes at one time and taking art class, singing lessons, and saxophone and guitar. I guess I was trying to catch up with all the lost time in the Navy and my secluded childhood. The dreams were alive and flowing from me like water from a well. I did this for four years, and then I hit a wall. I stopped one day, looked around and saw, I was one alone and all my friends were, well they were still my friends, but not there for me, nor was I inspired by them. My mission had gained me a bit of a following and a much better understanding of self and others, but I was still not inspired. Wait for a second, was it lack of inspiration, or lack of direction? Ahhh, right. For me, it was lack of direction, and I misunderstood. So, I took a weekend to write about it and sit in silence as I often do awaiting the voice to guide me. It took a few nights before I was able to be calm enough to hear it, but it came. The inner voice spoke very little but said, "focus on your career." Wait? I thought that's what I was doing.?? Oh, right, my acting career, right. I had been building myself or self-awareness so much I left the creative passion that gave me inspiration and fulfillment like no other. Two weeks later I was in rehearsal for what would become the most exposing and challenging theatrical play I would do to this day. I dropped all that I had been holding onto that made me feel superior in a vulnerable way and dove in with all of me. It turns out, I was looking outside myself and I allowed the outside energy in. That all dropped off as the play opened to excellent reviews. five months later, when we had last curtain call, we had garnished the LA weekly and LA critics choice awards. I was nominated for an Ovation award as well as LA weekly award for the best dramatic actor. But, that's not the point. The point is when you focus on you and your direction, goals, and visions, the rest comes. That play changed my life and my career. I booked two films from it, a TV show, hired a talent manager, received a letter from Robert Redford commending me on my performance. It was a turning point in my life and I had no idea going in. So, when you are seeking inspiration, ask yourself, is it inspiration, or direction you are seeking? Answer honestly and then whatever the choice is, dig down deep inside and begin to trust that choice.

Here we go! The Process begins now!

4 The Process

Welcome to the process. In this chapter, we will get dirty and dive deep into the brilliant parts of you. Some, you may not even know exist until now. Others, you may rediscover and define or give new meaning to. The process is the biggest part of this book, so unlike the first quick chapters, this one will take you into a more scenic journey that is sure to spark your creativity, awareness, power and hopefully inspire you to carry on. So, before we begin, I wanted to make sure you are ready for this. Have you been stuck or feeling stuck in a dead-end job? Have you longed to do something creative, like paint, sculpt, play music, or create your own store, shop or business? Okay, I'm hoping you answered yes to at least one subject on that list. This means you are in the right place and this process is about to change your life forever if you allow it. But, before that happens, don't you think you should know a little more about me? Why I wrote this book and how this code has helped others? No? Okay, then let us begin. Haha. I'll share a few thoughts and keep it simple. For me, the process began at an early age when I was 4. I was raised in a loud and sometimes violent household. Like most American kids at that time, I found ways to escape the violence and screaming. And, as you might know, we didn't have cell phones, personal computers, games of any kind to distract us, so the good ole imagination kicked in and it saved my life. I was a dreamer, still am, the only difference is today I live my dreams and back then they were just means of escape. But, I paid a price because I was avoiding my life and my truth. The truth was, I was afraid of my father and I ran away each day to find peace. Yes, this was a survival method and it got me out of the chaos, but it would come up in my later life to haunt me. The fact is, I shoved all my feelings down, stuffed my life into an invisible existence and was afraid of confrontation and expressing myself for a very long time. This is the basis of The Process Code. Because, as I've found in my life as a creative being, denying who I was and who I am are the keys to success. The little boy who dreamed is the same person who creates. Knowing what I know now and understanding the patterns that were formed in my youth I have dis-covered a way to layout the images from my past and pinpoint how they affected me, when and why. Through this process, you too will find that hero inside that has been with you since youth. As we gather information about you and your past, you will learn to quickly study and determine what works and what doesn't, What affects you still today and what has been blocking you from getting what you want, or deserve. Yes, deserve. we all deserve rewards, accolades, and acknowledgment. We all deserve what we wish for. Agree? So, to recap about me. I went through a horribly abusive childhood that destroyed my self-esteem. I was bullied in school, beaten down by those I looked up to, ridiculed by peers and told I was stupid. Yes, there were a lot of memories and over a decade of abuse daily. But, I survived it and not only survived, but I've also reached outside to look in and understand how and why releasing the old patterns and thoughts and dis-beliefs. I broke down the walls that were pretty thick. It wasn't easy and took some time, but I found my vulnerability while still remaining to keep my ability to stand my ground. Here's a good quote from one of my favorite acting coaches and mentors. This quote was repeated in class weekly and it affected my life in a positive way.

Remember, this was a question from the self-esteem test. Most of us care what others think of us. Right? I mean, that's why you're not successful, or as successful as you want to be. Correct? It's that worry about where you might fit in with your current peers, or friend groups. What your parents might think of you if you actually do something great with your life. Because, whatever you do when you are in alignment with your true passion or desire, you will be successful. You may not be aware of this success at the moment, but that's again why you are here. The fact I just wrote that made you more aware of it and will make you more aware of things as they come up. Do you still care what others think of you? Well, don't!

> *"Don't give a shit about what others think of you."* - Harry Mastrogeorge

Keep that one for later use too. You'll learn to tap into your power and you might even have to get a little angry to get that power back. After all, anger stems from the emotion of fear, or not understanding. So, in order to understand something we might get angry and in turn deal with the fear to create peace with it. Listen, it's a process, I didn't say this was easy and it's definitely not going to happen in a day or two. The good news is, it will happen and if you do the work it will happen as soon as you allow it.

Remember its a Process. The Process Code looks like this when you break it down.

1. Begin to uncover the past trauma, pain, fears that hold you in one place.
2. To release the old patterns and begin new ones.
3. To begin to live in balance and fearlessness, pursuing your goals.

Sounds simple enough right? That's only three steps to change all that is blocking you at this time. But, the reality is, it doesn't happen in one day or one session. For some it may take months, others, a couple of weeks. In general, or on average, we begin to see results from clients in about two weeks' time when they are working on their own. For fastest results, you can sign up for one on one sessions with me and speed up the process. I've had students/clients have results within the first hour or session. But, again the key is to KEEP going, keep moving forward in your own process. If you do not work well by yourself join a support group or one of our groups online. Or, you can book a session with me now, or volunteer to come on stage at our next event near you. The onstage work is limited in time, but gives you a free session and could jumpstart your process. Either way, we are here to support you through this. Now, what other books or authors do that? My goal or passion in this life and you can go back to my childhood and find this. My passion is to help others, period. I've been blessed with a wonderful and challenging career that has allowed me to spend countless hours reading, studying, rehearsing, practicing, learning, watching, listening and helping others for a very long time. It has taken me 4 years to write this book. There have been many almost titles and almost ideas for the book and yeah I even thought of being conventional and having 47 testimonials, 100 test subjects, etc, but that's not me. I've written this process workbook for you. For you to be able to easily relate, regardless of who you are, where you come from, or what you do in life. I want this book to be relatable to all. After all of my work and coaching and researching for the past 35 years, I believe we all share a common background, again regardless of heritage, ethnicity, social background, and/or geographical location. We all have this truth that we were born with and that's what we have to share with the world. That childlike spirit, it's essence and brilliance. We all have it or had it. The key is to use The Process Code to unlock the past in order to live your future.

Are you ready to jump in?

As we begin, lets begin with the goals, because we must have an end game, or goal know where we are going. What is your goal, or goals for this work? Goal examples: To get my dream job? To find happiness and peace in myself to live a comfortable lifestyle. or, to just let go of my past and face my fears. What is your goal (s)?_____

_____

_____

_____

_____

_____

_____

_____

_____

_____

"It's good to have an end to journey toward; but its the journey that matters in the end."–Ursula K. Le Guin

Do you have your first goal? Good, it may expand as you go, but let's keep it in the crosshairs as we move forward. Are you ready for this? Come on, no hesitation, we are about to get dirty in diving into your past to get to know them now and/or the future. But, we have to open the box or door a little bit further to allow the light in. Once, we have enough light, we will know it's safe to go into the past. So, imagine a door slightly open like the image here, with the sun shining through. Allow this to be a safe visual you can recall from time to time. Do you have yours? You can change the color of the door, the landscape, etc, whatever brings you happiness. You can take a few minutes to sketch out your own as well, we would like to see them, so if at all possible and you feel like sharing, please send them to us or post on our page. The links are provided at the back of this book or found on our website. www.TheProcessCode.com. Please share your drawings or sketches, this will help us understand you and your process better as well. Thank you. Now that you have your image, or are using ours, lock it in and know if you feel uncomfortable, you can resort back to it.

Here we go! What is stopping you, or blocking you in your life right now that keeps you from achieving your goal(s)? Again, try to pick one if there are many things, they will reveal themselves as we continue and you will learn the process to go back and do the same steps in each scenario. Let's say its FEAR. Fear of what? Success? Failure? (which are the same fear) Fear of beginning? Fear of getting what you want or what you visualize? Fear of what others might say? That's a big one. I was so afraid of what others thought of me, or would think of me as I grew up in a small town where everyone was competitive, and no one really had much of anything. It was small town politics and the haters were brutal. Even today I continuously get hit with jealous remarks on facebook, or hateful comments on my posts. I'll go back to the quote from earlier in this chapter. *"Don't give a shit about what others think of you."* You have to remember this is about YOU, your journey to a better you and a better way of living. You'll have to face diversity regardless, but to not do anything, is a loss. You've come this far, so lets keep moving forward. YOU GOT THIS! Fear, or no fear we need to move forward. So, what is blocking you at this time in your life? _____

_____

_____

_____

_____

_____

_____

_____

_____

_____

_____

_____

_____

_____

*"The thing you fear most has no power. Your
fear of it is what has the power. Facing the truth
really will set you free."* - Oprah Winfrey

Now that you have written and committed to the
first subject, we will learn to dis-cover and un-cover and
find out where it lies in your past and now. We will learn
to shed light on it and take away its bellicose hold on you.
The process code #1. Remembering the past. Before we can
get to the goal, we need to fix a few things. Code number 1
is to determine your patterns. Remember we briefly talked
about patterns in the beginning? What are your patterns and
how to change, or fix them? Here's the first set of questions
to dis-covering your patterns. Now, again, I do not know
your goal, or what's blocking you, so not every question may
pertain directly to you and/or your circumstance, but I bet
they do affect you.

Question 1: I have good ideas, but I often don't follow
through with them. True? False? **#2**: In the past I have given

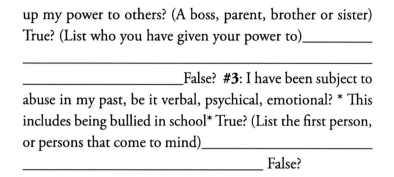

up my power to others? (A boss, parent, brother or sister) True? (List who you have given your power to)_____

_____False? **#3**: I have been subject to abuse in my past, be it verbal, psychical, emotional? * This includes being bullied in school* True? (List the first person, or persons that come to mind)_____
_____ False?

Feedback from the first three questions. If you said true to question one, this connects to the fear we mentioned and know you are in the right place. If you said false, I'd like to question your intentions or your honesty with self. Are you aware of your ideas? If so, are you just not acknowledging them at this moment? If so, go back and change your answer. If you are not aware, I challenge you to reflect on this. What do you think of most in life? What gets you up in the morning? I don't mean what literally gets you up, I mean WHAT DO YOU STRIVE FOR? HUNGER FOR? These types of thoughts and/or feelings are the ideas and drive I'm asking about. What made you pick up this book? Now you are getting it. These are the tools that we weren't taught in school or life in general.

MY PROMISE: I Josh Carmichael, the author of this book, promise to not only give you permission to feel and dream, but to give you the starter kit of tools to begin to fill up your own toolbox, which in turn will allow you to advance, grow and change the way you live in your current situation. That's my promise, to take you on this literary journey with gifts abound! I promise. And, if you know me or know of me, I fulfill my promises. But, these promises can't be fulfilled if you quit, or don't complete the work. I encourage you to give it a minimum of two weeks after you have finished and doing the morning exercises before you decide.

Now that you have my promise, why don't you make one to yourself. For example; I promise to finish this book. I promise to be honest with myself no matter how difficult it may be. I promise to allow myself to grow. There are a few samples, now your turn. I PROMSE:_____

_____

_____

_____

_____

_____

Feel better? Let's get back to this.. I hope you feel like I'm reading and doing this with you, as that's my intention. I know this process works, as it's worked for me and many others, so I'm going on this journey with you, to support you and be there on the other side when you achieve your dreams and goals.

Question #2 Answer. If you answered yes, and I'm guessing most of you did. Who have you given your power to and are you still with this person? By the way, if you are in a volatile relationship, or feel you are in danger in any way, PLEASE call for help. You can reach out to your local hotline now, or connect to one of these. www.justanswer.com/relationships, www.safehelpline.org. Make that change now. We want to make sure you seek the help you need if you are in need at this time. As you move forward with this process you will begin to gain back that power and you will have more awareness and strength to hopefully take on your challenges with passion!

When, or how long ago did you give your power away?_____Do they have an affect on your life now?_____ If yes, are you aware of that affect? Let's say you are afraid of them and or what they might do if you act out. If this is the case, you can trust now that this will begin to change the way you think now. Perhaps you are already. Imagine your life without them in it for a moment. What does that look like? Knowing you have more control of how they affect you now. What's it like when you are free from them, not in a harmful way, but a free spirit way. Visualize yourself in the now living the life you desire. Are they a part of it? Yes, I asked you to think of life without them, but I'm asking if they are still showing up? This means you have more work to do in order to free yourself of them even in thought. You don't yet believe you are capable of being on your own. So, where are you in the now? What are you doing, what kind of car are you driving, or boat you are sailing on? How do you feel? Write it out here. GO!_____

_____

_____

_____

_____

_____

_____

_____

_____

_____

_____

_____

_____

What you just wrote was the first steps in the power or laws of attraction. Something I use in my life daily. *What you think about you bring about.* What you visualize you attract. Now, I used that as an example of what can be and also as a mirror to what is. You see your life now is all of the old energy of what you've been attracting. The old patterns, the past, the history you've kept in your closet like those boxes you refuse to throw out. Oh yes, we will clean out your clutter in figurative and literal means. Now, that you can see the direct connection to the future and the present moment or the past leading up to now, lets continue.

Let's say you selected someone close to you, a parent or parental figure that has been the one you gave your power to. If it is from childhood and most of our issues are, then you are in the majority and honestly, there wasn't much you could do about it back then. Right? So why beat yourself up about it? It wasn't your fault, you didn't cause it. Even if you think you might have, you were a child and it was part of your lessons in life to get you to this point. The abuse we gather as children is the so what of our lives and the past or history that truly affects almost everything in our adult life, from relationships to career, job, habits, weight issues, eating habits, depression, anxiety, and the big one TRUST.

Here's a little insight, since we are getting to know one another. My father was a raging alcoholic and both verbally and physically abusive to me and my sister. I can only speak for myself as I went through years of daily verbal bashing from ages 5-14. When I was fourteen I got a job. My restricted drivers' license permitted me to go to and from school and to and from work, so I was gone from home a lot. I worked after school, so I wouldn't have to see him.. But, I wouldn't realize the effects he had on me until one night when he violently beat me. I somehow was able to drive myself to my mother's home. She took one look at me and we were off to the hospital. I was 19 and legally an adult so no charges were filed and I was lucky to not have had any serious or life-threatening injuries. But, the scars that would rise in their favor have lasted since. It took me 4 years away in the US NAVY and a lot of time in the gym to get enough courage to face my monster, my abuser. I was 24 when I finally stood before him and I'll never forget that moment. I could see the shame and guilt as I approached him outside of his home. At first, he ignored my words until I said: "Stop walking away from me, I'm talking to you!" He stopped and clenched his fists as if we were going to battle again, only this time I was prepared. He replied with a simple "Go ahead, what is so damned important?" my eyes seemed fixated on his fists, as I said " What are you going to hit me again? Go ahead, it will be your last time you ever do." This seemed to have affected him in a way I wasn't ready for. He took a beat, bowed his head and then when his eyes met mine, they were softer, kinder. His hands relaxed. He said, you're right son, go ahead. Huh? I was right? I hadn't even expressed what was boiling inside. I was right? I was speechless for a moment, then I said, with a long pause as I stared at this man who now seemed so small in stature to me and said… "Uh, you know what you did was wrong, and it made me very angry inside. For the past 4 years I've been planning ways to beat you up, or badly hurt you so that you felt what I did, and then one day I realized, you saved my life. By beating me to the ground, you lit the match inside of me that would cause a fire to survive and that anger and fear of never allowing anyone to do that again was the best thing you've ever done for me. And so, I came back to first hurt you, beat you and win, but then I saw that that wasn't the answer, the bigger answer was… Well, I thank you, dad, thank you for making me a man"… Then silence. He turned to walk into his shop and said, "I gotta get back to work, you finished?" "Yeah, I'm done." and with that, he walked away. We never talked about that subject again. And As I walked back to my car and headed for the airport I wondered what he did when those garage doors closed behind him? Did he cry? Did he fall to his knees, or did he just move on and actually do his work? I'll never know, but I can share this. I've never been bullied since. That was my beginning, at 24 and I've made it my path to help others since moving to Los Angeles in 1990. I'm a small-town kid from Kansas and I know if I can do it, I can teach it to you, or give you the tools to find it.

Shall we go back to you? I'm hoping my truth has helped. You can do this too. Okay, does it feel like I'm coaching you? I'm trying. :) You have no idea what it means to me that you are here now reading this and taking these tools into your future. Regardless of how far you go with them, your life is changing and you are growing as we go. I'm so excited for you.

Carry on.

There are so many ways to address your abuser, or the one to whom you have listed here as the energy sucker. Let's get back to how you feel. What is the feeling when you are around this person?_____

_____

_____

_____

_____

"There is no passion to be found playing small—
in settling for a life that is less than the one you
are capable of living." - Nelson Mandela

Okay, now lets tap into where that feeling lives in your body. If this affects your body physically you might feel your body tense up, or freeze. We humans are emotional beings who have created many years of blocks and a lot of stuffing of feelings/emotions due to good ole life living. Depending on your age and how many years you've gone without dealing. Well, congrats!! you've reached a time in life for something new. And it's never too late to start. There's no age limit on this. THINK BACK–I want you to think back for a moment again to when the feeling of loss of power began. Were you aware of it at that moment? If you were, what did you do to stop it? Nothing right? Okay, what would you have said if given the chance now? _____

_____

_____

_____

_____

_____

How did that feel when you just expressed it? Were you biting your nails? Clinching your fists? Where was the tension in your body? Make note of this. It's important to fist.png ¬know where and what your patterns are even in rage or frustration.

IT'S OKAY TO FEEL EMOTIONS! There I said it again. It's okay to feel. This is the beginning of accepting you and who you are as a wonderful feeling and emotional soul. We all deserve to feel. it's our happy place, even if there's sadness, the fact that we have the ability to feel such a rush of anything. Hopefully the good will outweigh the not so good and it will IF that's what you want to attract.

Think again of the red door, or your door and the light coming in. The light representing love and light itself. Allow it to flow over you and make you feel alive. Be grateful and thankful that you have made a very strong first step.

Look, we all know most self-help books talk about the results from clients and sell you on a theory. I'm right here with you teaching you The Process Code and how to use the tools to navigate through to a brighter and happier life course. I believe we ALL deserve more from life and it is up to us to get it. But, because of the insecure people of our past and the trials and tribulations of society, we have taken the brick and mortar and built up walls around our inner self. A shield if you will. A mask. Do you agree? I do. I had to strip off the masks I wore getting through life as a scared and wounded soul. Makes you kinda pissed off doesn't it? It does me, let's be honest, there's a part that gets angry and blames society on the fact that we feel we should have been protected. Right? There's a tantrum in there that cries out why!? Where were the safety nets and guards to hold us safe and console us when we were all alone and scared? Get pissed off, let it out! Scream if you have to! Or, do this. Stand up or do it from where you are seated at this moment and take a deep breath in through your nose. Hold it for a few seconds and tighten up your entire body. Clinch those fist. Tighten your butt cheeks, toes, and stomach. tighten, tighten, tighten! Hold it, hold it, hold it for a few more seconds and RELEASE! Exhale and relax. Whoo, feel that? Feels good, doesn't it? You just released a lot of tension. Well done!

We didn't have people there to protect us, because we didn't have people around us that new any better, or knew this process or code. They hadn't and most likely haven't done the work themselves. Yeah, that would be great and in a perfect world might be normal, but that doesn't happen does it? No. And the fact that life has obstacles is well part of life. But, think about this. If YOU are doing this work now and you are growing and changing right now at this very moment, think about this. If, you are changing the patterns from the past now and you are about to become a parent, or already are one, or a teacher, or want to coach others and/or affect others in some way, then wow! Think about how much better you are going to be. Think of how you will handle situations differently, more aware and maybe more calmly. Because.

"Life is a mess. It has always been a mess. We are not going to change it. Our job is to straighten out our own lives." - Joseph Campbell

Mr. Campbell was a wonderful professor and mythologist. He wrote several powerful books, to include The Hero with a Thousand faces. If, you don't know of him, or haven't heard of him, please give him a read when you can.

I am giving you these inserts as we go to motivate you. And to allow something to happen in you as you digest the emotions as they may have a greater effect on some more than others. So, I'm taking into consideration the time and the wave of the process. Remember, each expression, phrase, and direction has a meaning and purpose.

EXCUSES–How many of you are making excuses for your life? Or for the lack of having what you want? Maybe you are making excuses for the person you are living with or in a relationship with because of the issues we've talked about earlier. Fear? Let me ask you, are you procrastinating in your life thinking that you need to have your finances in order to, or to have the right job in place to? That if you can just get ahead long enough to take a breath and then you can make that bold move. ?? Correct? Those are excuses and avoidance of the truth. The truth is, if you are waiting 3 weeks, 3 years, or even 1 week, you may never get there. WHY? Because you are missing the now. Today is the start of something new and its all-new information. Do you see where you are making excuses? This part of the pattern is a real tough one to get people to change. It's the one we are most likely to ignore because it's so close to home. If I take responsibility for my actions? I'll be responsible? Oh, SHIT! That's scary, right? To actually take responsibility for yourself? How many of you have done something wrong, broke a window, stole from someone, lied to get out of something and never took responsibility for it? All of you right? I mean, come on we were all kids once and we called them white lies, or fibs. They didn't seem to harm us or those around us. Right? Wrong! They are or could be part of what's bothering you now, believe it or not. The very reason you are making excuses now could be because you got away with it then. Its no different from a criminal, yeah crimes seem way worse and the violent acts are not what I'm referring to. It's the action of continuing to lie and withhold or cheat or betray others, are excuses to avoid dealing with the truth. So, are you lying to yourself? If you're avoiding or making excuses you are. You're not allowing the truth to be your own and take responsibility for what you desire. Understand? I was a terrible lier when I was young. I once was shooting my bb gun in the yard and it ricochets off a rock and shattered the neighbor's old car window. when my parents first asked me I lied and said I didn't know anything about it. Three days later as it ate away at my insides, and hearing my mother teaching in my head, to be honest, I told her and asked how I could pay for it, as I held up my piggy bank full of pennies. I felt so much relief and my mother and father must have worked it out as the neighbors said, thank you for being honest, it was an old car, and I never paid for it, nor did I ever shoot my gun around that area again. Good lesson though. I was nine.

Guess what, by doing the power exercises, you have already begun. Now, it's time to look a little more closely, or deeper into the why or what you are avoiding. We know by association that the abuse from our past is or has put us into a victim mentality to start with and it has taken up until now to realize, that we are not alone, that we are capable of changing the patterns and, we have the ability to take back our power from them regardless if they are living or not. This is YOUR TIME!

Stop the excuses, stop avoiding and begin to allow the truth to emerge again. See that door again, open it further. The light will protect you and wake you up. Trust what you already know. Begin to accept that trust as the now, or the moment and hold it for a few minutes. Feel it as it washes over you. Can't feel it? Then just imagine yourself in perfect harmony with your goals.

Words of association; decision or choice? Say those words out loud. Decision and then choice. Can you feel the difference? Choice to me seems happier and easier with less resistance. You? _____

Entertain and possess. How do each of these make you feel?_____

_____
_____

> *Believe vs Doubt.* This should be an easy
> one. Do you feel the different energy?

I am doing vs I am thinking about it. Again, an easy one. But, I want you to begin to question the phrases and terms you use in everyday life. How many words and their inflection affect your life? You'll be surprised how many you use and how often. You'll begin to hear the excuses, or see the lack of commitment to the action of.

Begin to analyze yourself and you'll begin to hear it in others. You don't have to correct them just yet, even though you might want to. Hold onto this until you truly have it down.

Hey, let's go over something again, because I have this feeling you are feeling overwhelmed and ready to bail on me, or shut down even further, instead of knocking down the walls. Are you listening to me? The Process Code, is a process and you can't expect instant results, although you are already feeling something and feeling dis-comfort or perhaps a stirring in the body, and if you are like most people I've worked with, I can feel you shut down, turn off and distract yourself with something to do, or suddenly remember you didn't put the dishes away. Okay, that's old pattern again and it's not going to help you. The dishes will wait. The key is or question is at this point, DO YOU WANT TO GROW? Are you ready to allow more joy, more happiness, more excitement and more positive energy throughout? Are you ready to feel better, feel healthier, increase your level of trust, and interest in others? That's what you are here to do right? I thought so, now let's RAISE YOUR VIBRATION!

I'm still here with you, every step of the way and don't think I'm bailing on you, or talking down to you if this seems to be holding you up. I'm taking into consideration those of you who are waffling a bit or are new to this work. It's about being fair to all and knowing and understanding that we ALL have a voice and a presence that deserves to be heard. So, let's hear yours. Here's a little pep talk to boost your butt up and get you pumped and ready for the next steps or actions.

small switch

Flip the Switch!

Remember, that person or persons that have talked down to you all your life, or as far back as you can remember? Yep, you know the ones and they may be doing it still today. Those people are the ones who are most in pain. Let's wrap our minds around that for a moment. It's not you, it's their issues. If you are the bullying person, this will affect you too, or if you have hurt others to make yourself feel better. It doesn't work, does it? It ALWAYS comes back to the one who is angry or being mean. And, it comes back in various forms, like illness, cancer, accidents, and you'll see them tear apart their families and friends. If that person is YOU, please take a moment and ask yourself why you have been so upset, or hurting so much that you have to blame others, or take it out on them? Why? Take a few minutes and analyze yourself and your thoughts. Now quickly make a switch.. See the light switch on the wall? Pick any of them, just look at one and imagine it's the switch to your thoughts and flip it either way up or down. With that switch, it changes the polarity as it does in electricity and you can simply change the way you think that quickly. Yes, you can! Go ahead flip that switch! Did it work? If it did, you will understand how easy it is to change. If it didn't work try saying this as you try it again. I know, you are resistant because you didn't get this WOW moment the first time, but maybe we need to add a little to it. Say this, "I'm taking control of my thoughts and turning on new energy that allows me to vibrate at a higher frequency and helps me to understand myself better." Remember this is about you not them, so think about how to better yourself. That's the goal here. That's The Process

Code. Go ahead do it. For those who are not having this issue, hold tight as we go through this for others. Patience is part of your issue in life and so we are practicing that as we read and wait to move forward. This can help you all in some way because we all have moments of feeling down or sad or angry. Use this exercise to flip the switch and let the light shine now. Maybe, the door, your door just opened a little bit more allowing things to become more bright.Are we all caught up?

The difference between a feeling and a thought: What's the difference? This may seem like a trivial question, but I bet a lot of you don't know. So, here's the difference. Feelings come first in most cases, we feel something, often called the gut instinct. Feelings represent demand or action. Thoughts are the managers of the feelings. Often, we think ourselves out of a feeling and create a solution before the feeling is ever met, or realized. We need to learn to combine these two in harmony so the thoughts resonate with the feelings and allow them to be managed openly. Feelings are emotional, thoughts are more controlled efforts to understand something or rationalize them. When I ask you to feel, I want to you think back, yes think back that little child who had feelings and desires before words ever got in the way. Allow your feelings to be undisturbed and notice when you begin to question them and how you speak for them and analyze them. Now you know. The more you feel and trust those feelings, I mean really trust them, you'll see how fast your life will change and how many new experiences you'll have. Feelings are what make us feel great. Thoughts are like the map and feelings are the transportation that gets us there. The fuel. Fuel your thoughts.

Now, that the light is on, the door is opened
a bit further, so let's ask a few questions.

> 1. How do you feel right now? I'm not asking what you think, I'm asking what you feel?

So, before you answer here's a list of the 5 acting emotions.
1. Fear–a feeling of being afraid, scared.
2. Anger–feeling angry

3. Sadness

4. Love

5. Joy Love is a heightened feeling of joy and is alone in its own category as you feel the love you feel compassion.

Congratulations, you've just completed step one in the process. This mantra or motto will begin to settle in your skin and your being and begin to work it's magic as if you didn't know it was there. You are a creator and a powerful being, all of you. We just added another tool to the toolbox. It's called COURAGE. Well done, let's move on.

What, your toolbox doesn't look like this? It's an emotional Toolbox :)

The Process Step Two:
Believing your own word and worth. If you are like me, and no I'm not going into an entire soliloquy right now, but if you are like me it may take some time to own up to your belief in yourself and your word, or new words. You don't think words are powerful? Oh, you are about to find out just how much power they have over you. You'll see how your body reacts to certain words and what nervous conditions or anxieties they may bring with them. Are you aware of this? Let's do a few check-ins to see where you are with them.

Failure - How does this word affect you? Do you feel any tension in your body? Does it connect to you at all?

Fear - How about this one?

Weakness - and this one?

Coward - ??

Hero-?

Survivor - Does this connect to you? Where in your body? Do you bite your nails? Or feel tension anywhere? I get it in my neck and stomach mostly.

Shallow - I'm not talking about the song title here from "A Star is Born."

Desperate - Anything?

Beautiful - Does this one feel good?

Chaos - ??

Powerful - I hope this one sparks some movement in the creative juices.

Safe - ?

Lost - Anything?

Alone - ??

Successful - I'm hoping this feels good too.

Vulnerable - ??

As you look these over and maybe come back to this on a different day, give it a few weeks, you'll find different answers. My point is, we are constantly changing and based on how well we slept, what foods we eat and how healthy you feel at the moment. The weather can be a factor too if you are very sensitive like me. So, was there a commonplace in your body that you felt tension or stiffness? Did you notice a pattern of who the words were associated with? Another person? Yourself? How many made you feel great? How many had zero effect on you? Are you being honest with your emotions? Okay, on a scale of 1-10, 10 being the highest, how high is your self-esteem right now?_____

How about your belief in yourself?_____ And do you believe you are worthy or have self-worth? Scale it 1-10?_____ What if, I said you were amazing right now and doing excellent work? I feel there's some doubt, and I'm excited about that too. Because that's the dis-comfort or uncomfortable place that pushes us to grow. That doubt can be a great tool to use to motivate one's self. The more and more you do the check-ins and ask questions of yourself and analyze the words that slip from your tongue, the more you will see the level of effect from old patterns and the past. Do you see any patterns yet? _____ Have you begun to feel them in your body and are you ready to release the old energy for good?_____ I hope you wrote something like "Hell yes!"

Believing in yourself and self-worth are the CONFI-DENCE building tools that we can now add to your toolbox. Yes, your very own egg toolbox. :) Regardless of what your toolbox looks like, you can begin using Confidence now and believing in The Process Code even more. By accepting the new memories or connections to the words and feelings they have over you, you can again flip the switch if need be and alter the effect of them. Vulnerability; Please allow me to touch on this one for a moment. When I first began opening up, I was told I was vulnerable by an acting coach. He praised me for it matter of fact, but I was uncomfortable with it, as I had an association that vulnerability meant weakness. Weakness meant weak and soft. So, needless to say, I was offended by this accusation, until it was explained to me in more detail. Vulnerability in the way it was being used and as I use it here is a form of understanding and openness.

A strength in having the ability to drop your guard and be able to pretend in an acting exercise, or just be in real life. Literally, word bullets can't hurt you once you accept and adapt to this behavior and understanding. It's pure pleasure and strength wrapped into one. So, for you macho guys out there, and if you've seen me, you'll know I'm considered a big macho guy too, a mans man, etc, listen up! Being tough and angry and violent isn't strong. That's the weakness because it goes against everything you are learning here. How to understand and express your *FEELINGS*. Why do you want to punch the guy at the bar who accidentally bumped into you? Why are you loud and angry when your girlfriend says she wants to go home, or even deeper, doesn't want to be with you anymore? You get upset and act out at times, you punch the wall, or slam the door or throw your phone. Yeah, ever been in that situation? Ring a bell? Sound familiar? Okay, let's deal with this one for a moment. That anger is heated up because of what? Fear! You're afraid and don't know how to react. So, it becomes dramatic, Ladies this is for you too because we know women can get heated just as much as guys. That fear is because you don't know what you feel. You get anxiety because the circumstances are now presented and out of your comfort zone. The alarm inside that hits the FLAME ON button and we are hot! right? Well, that fear can be defused very simple if you learn how to understand your feelings, like instead of punching the wall, you say, "Wow that really hurts my feelings, why do you say that?" The other person in return might say "You embarrassed me and I think it's rude, so I'm not comfortable here and want to leave." Fair enough. Then the guy or girl who's defensive could do a couple of things. First, apologize for their behavior, or two acknowledge they did this and say perhaps you misunderstood me when I said that. Get it? I'm telling you, it can be resolved and figured out without conflict 100% of the time. If we can all just learn the tools to understand our pain. That's why the first thing we learn in the past pain because it's got a good hold on your future and this just shed more light one it. It's fading out fast and you are learning The Process Code quicker than you think. Well, I bet that stood your ears up for a moment. Huh? Come on Josh, you're saying that by learning how I feel and being in touch with the general feelings, can change my anger? Yep, that's what I'm saying and I'm also telling you from a physically strong man to another, vulnerability is the answer. Why? Because it allows you the clarity to be more aware, awake and present in the situation at hand. Again, that higher vibration. It's also connected to a great intelligence level within the self. If you can master the emotions and master them well, you will not only not attract violence any longer, you will attract much higher energy of peace and love and happiness and wealth and abundance. That's emotional intelligence.

I've learned to defuse any situation and have counseled several couples with this for relationships. It's called COMMUNICATION.
Note: People will tell you all you need to know if you just listen. Confidence and communication, add them to your egg toolbox.

Step three:

How many of you are struggling with letting go of the past at this time? Do you feel resistant to change? What is going on in that active mind of yours? How do I know? Because I know how difficult it can be to take on a new pattern and/or to change an old one. I also know how much it may scare you as it did me at one time to take that leap into the unknown and trust this actually works. already, I have given you the fast track tools to change and awareness. But, I know about now, and let's call this day three of the book, you are (if you are like me) struggling between letting go of the past and understanding the process. Correct? If this is not you, you can proceed to the next chapter. If this does relate to you, then let's air it out. I can give you insight from here. So, what are you feeling? Anxiety? Fear? Okay, if one or both of these are accurate, let's go back a moment to do a check-in. Have you been doing the positive affirmation or motto work daily? If not and you are rushing to get through this book so you can say you completed it, then you are going about this with the wrong intention. Please don't be like me here and read the book to display on your trophy case as I have. Go back and yes I know I hate that word. Go back and do it again. It's familiar to rehearsal when they say "back to one." I'm always like, I got it already, let's move forward. But, in comparison to, wait. What's your favorite movie?_____

_____ How many times have you seen it?_____ Okay, did you see things in it the second or third time, that you did not in the first? That's the point when you go back and repeat an action or steps, you not only learn more, see more, understand more, you also are one step closer to making it a habit. Do it 5 or 6 more times and it will be locked in. Did that help? Okay, now carefully, let us try and uncover that fear again. There's a lot of it, isn't there? Yes, I know, it repeats itself taking on different visuals or situations. Fear let's break it down. FEAR: An unpleasant often strong emotion caused by anticipation or awareness of danger.

> *"What man does not understand he fears; and what he fears, he tends to destroy."* - William Butler Yeats

Fear is something we have given power to. Why the very mention of the word makes us tense up, doesn't it? Fear. That's the past. Now I want you to say, I feel it and I'm not afraid. I know it's a negative word in general, but we are going to bring more light to it once again so we can make FEAR become positive. Yes, imagine fear or fear-based terms now becoming positive. Remember, what you think about you bring about. So, let's see fear as the match that lights the candle to shine a light on our path, our journey trail. Fear is now a good term, fear is now a match or light itself. Can you see it? Okay, how does that feel in your body? Doesn't it feel like progress? The light illuminates the path to carry on, move forward and shine. Yay! We now have a positive action for that ole buddy of ours. You know, our childhood, or during our childhood, we knew intuitively but we didn't have the voice or perhaps words yet to express when we felt we were being wronged, or conned, mistreated. We knew it felt wrong and if you were sexually abused, well that builds a different wall and is a tough one to overcome if you give in to that fear of it. What I am digging into here, it the facts that, if we can go back in our minds of those tragedies and pain and abuse, or abandonment and realize it all happened for a reason. I'm not saying it was right, oh no, nor am I suggesting it was our fault, no, no, no, not at all. What, I'm saying, is if you can go back and look at it in a way as I did when I confronted my father and thanked him for making me a man. You see, I didn't mention the effects that moment had on my life. My life, after that, changed forever and I didn't think of the beating or abuse much more and I certainly did not give it any energy or attention. I made it a positive as we have just done with fear. Do you see? If you change the way you look at things, the things you look at change. Again, over the years we have been told, fed drama and news media that creates more drama and fear within us. That's the purpose of it, to keep us scared and asleep so we won't question or wake up and realize our true meaning, or have power in some way. Well, think about this, we built up bigger walls because we have been infected by things around us.

If you are like me, you weren't born into privilege and groomed for success. If you were, well you must have gone against the grain or uncovered the truth of your heritage and family. Good job. If you are like me, we weren't given the secrets to success and abundance. We weren't fed creative thoughts, ideas, or were surrounded by those who did. We were cut off from that society and left to figure it out on our own. Not to say that cannot happen from being from an affluent family. I knew several kids growing up and in my teens, that seemed more lost and had a lack of self-esteem. I found that the abandonment issues were and have remained the strongest aspect of this journey. It seems we all felt like we got left out in some way, or at some time in our lives and we have this urge to fit in, be heard, or be close to others. Is this you? If so, do you find yourself never wanting to be alone and have a need for others to need you? Or, there's that empty feeling inside when you are not performing or acting, telling jokes, or being the class clown as they say? Is this you?

Abandonment; I'm highlighting this one because of its such a common issue with people of all ages. Abandonment comes up most frequently in relationships and decides what role we give to the other person. If you have parental abandonment, you may give your spouse, or girlfriend/boyfriend the role of protector of all things and trust they can save you from abandonment. You check-in by either asking them to never leave or by acting out for attention to ensure they never do. But, what typically happens? You end the relationship, right? You destroy the good, to avoid what your subconscious already knows. That if they leave you cannot handle that much emotional feeling, so you end it and make them the bad guy to justify our actions. Right? Then what happens? You find yourself alone and if you are like me, you wake up one morning and you realize the pattern you thought was to protect you, has now destroyed all that was good and you are what? Left alone. Right? Yeah, this has been a big one for me most of my life and I can trace back the patterns to my father and the way in which he would set me up for disappointment. My parents never abandoned me, but they left me thinking it could happen at any moment. My father would give me presents and then take them away, just about the time I got to like the present or was getting joy from it, I would come home and it would be gone. For example, he brought home a brand new motorcycle for me one day. if you are like me, you love motorcycles. This one was my favorite and I must have had it for about a year when I came home one day and it was gone. When I asked my father, he said: "Ah, you didn't need it anymore." What was I to do? He was the boss. This went on and on throughout my life and so I began to not trust anyone would stick around and feared others would leave me once I started to get close to them, or they would be taken away. You see, a perfect example of patterns and how they affect our lives. So, how did I break it? Well, I stopped buying disposable things. Lol. Half kidding, but true. No, I realized when I took the power back from my father, and I did (actually still do) check-ins with myself, I began to understand it wasn't them, it was me and my lack of self-esteem and self-worth. That, I didn't feel worthy of love or being loved, yet it was the very thing that drove me. At first, when I had a lack of understanding, I sought love by the masses. I thought by performing and showing off, that people would love me and I felt it would be enough love to sustain me. Boy, was I mistaken? I, like some of you perhaps was running. I was running from my own self and my own fears. Much like you may feel or have felt in the past. And, again, even though there were self-help books and some great ones, there was nothing that could affect me enough to change this. Damnit! I searched, read, sought out, hung out in the Bodhi tree (A book store in Los Angeles), drank healing teas, took meditation classes, did yoga, practiced Buddhism, love and light classes, saw psychics, readers, did native American sweat lodges, attended pow-wows and grew my own kombucha mushroom. Nothing helped! And let me be clear about something here. I have never been into drugs or the use of any substance to alter my state of mind. I loved the feeling and I wanted more of it. So, how did I change? I just gave up on the control over something that truly had no control over me. I said to myself. "So what. What if they do leave, or go away, what if others hate me, or don't like me? I don't care, because I don't need someone else to make me feel happy and I don't need the applause from others to make me feel successful. I have me and I'm happy with that." And that was pretty much it. Oh sure the applause feels good and it's great to be appreciated, but think of how much better it feels when you are WHOLE! When you are truly being who you are and you feel it in your feet and your clothes and the way you walk, dress, laugh, eat, live and sleep. You'll see it as a reflection in your relationships and business deals. Your clients will respect you more and you will become a winner if you weren't before. You'll also feel so much more appreciation for life. To get there is to let go of the past.

Step three. Accepting the new patterns and owning your self-esteem, or ego.

"When I believe in something, I fight like hell for it." - Steve McQueen

BELIEVE

5 The Panel

The panels are those people and things or voices you hear, that we spoke of briefly before. The panel is the imaginary beings you've created in your mind over time to stop you, or to cause you to question yourself. We all have them or have had them in our lives, it could be from a mother who was afraid for herself and cast that onto you as a child. "Don't go too far, don't fall off your bike, don't stay up to watch scary movies, ' be careful you might get hurt, or you might break your leg, or lose a tooth." all of these create doubt and they are all negative reactions. Note: Anytime you use the words don't, can't, won't or quit, you are attracting more negatives or the things you just spoke of. Negative words have an effect on you and here are a few examples in general terms to understand them a little better. Here's what I learned as I was instructing my two sons when they were young. Instead of being like my parents and putting fear into them by screaming "Don't!" I realized that made them freeze and didn't teach them anything or didn't give them a positive outlook. So, I would say things like " Hey son, I need your help over here, can you help me?" I said this as I saw they were about to walk off the porch steps or feared they were in danger in some way. Now granted, it takes a lot more concentration as a parent and awareness of your children, but isn't that our job or duties as a parent? I'm not saying I'm the best father or know everything, as you will soon read. I made mistakes too, but it's the process of dealing with them that changed for me. So, I would not only make them feel important or included, I would actually involve them in something of more interest. It could be as simple as finding the remote to the television so they could watch baby Einstein. The fact was, I didn't put them in a place of shock or panic. Matter of fact, my oldest son, when he was 6 followed a stranger out of a store and did this while I had turned around to pay for my items. About 30 seconds worth and he was gone. When I saw he was missing I panicked and ran toward the doors, moments later, he ran by from outside the store with tears ins eyes. He was afraid and I quickly grabbed him and asked him what happened. I calmed him, even though I was panicked and scared. I thought I lost him. As we talked about it, we came to an agreement to hold hands and to make sure we had eye contact with one another from now on. But, I never made him feel bad about his choice, I just gave him the tools to change it and realize what he had done. In his case, he simply followed a man with a blue shirt. I happened to be wearing a blue shirt that day too. It was a common or general mistake. Let's just say it never happened again and he was more aware. Now, what if I had gotten angry or expressed my anger because I was afraid? That could have caused scars internally that we all have. Well, I just made an assumption, but If you are reading this and doing the work, there must be some kind of conflict, right? The more you release the past, the more distant the echoes of the panel will be. Just remember to acknowledge them as they come up and know they do not have any power over you any longer.

6. Love and Light

There was a time when we look back into our past and we remember those moments of love and light. Do you remember? I can. I remember my first kiss and the rush of feelings with it. I remember my first puppy and the love and laughter I got as he ran around the house like a crazy puppy. I remember my first love with a car, actually for me it was a 1947 chevy truck, but still a crush. Even though my life was chaotic as a child, I still was able to see some light and experience love or the feelings of love at a very early age. Of course, we all remember our first real crush or love. Right? What was yours? Knowing whatever type of lifestyle you had, good, bad, rich or poor, I bet you experienced some familiar feelings of love and light. The best thing about them when we were young, is we were realizing them for the first time and had no true understanding of the emotions, or feelings, but we did feel something, correct? If you are like me, being a dreamer, I would get lost in the idea of this new feeling of love lasting forever. It was a great way to escape the real-time mundane reality I was living then. It felt like movie love and I found myself drifting in and out of the romantic vision from an early age. I chuckle inside as I see myself in a golden wheat field walking as if I'm in slow motion and the climactic music surrounds me. I'm running toward someone as they are running to me, and then it stops as my hat flies from the gusts of wind and I am stumbling over my feet in order to catch it. That's one good way to stop a dream sequence. HaHa. And so we grow older and somehow we lose touch with that little boy or girl energy we once had. Those dreams fade into work schedules, classes, responsibilities and well, life. But, you do remember those feelings right? Okay, so now the goal is to recapture them and again use the tools here to unblock those feelings and drop the walls that have muddied our visions of them. We have to become childlike again. There are many quotes, theories, and books written o the subject of youth and I'm sure you know this quote by one of the greatest ever.

"Youth is wasted on the young." - George Bernard Shaw

Shaw was not only a prolific playwright, but he also won the Pulitzer Prize for literature in 1925 and an Oscar in 1938. The question remains, was our youth wasted when we were young? I think not. I believe and I hope you will too as you unravel and reveal your youth as the breeding ground for who you are today. That you'll begin to see parallels that reflect and mirror you in the same likeness all these years later. Unless you are in your youth reading this, then you will still need to go back to younger you, in the latency period perhaps. According to Freud, this period would begin around age 5 and go until puberty, or 15-16. For me, I felt it's greatest effects from 10-14. You may have experienced different times or ages. It's a personal thing, because of where we grow up and the culture that surrounds our youth has a direct effect on how quickly we process things and evolve, or mature. I personally was a late bloomer and can understand certain aspects of that due to the middle of the united states in which I was present at that time. Our city was small, the culture was behind the east and west coasts. Our way of thinking and everyday living were prehistoric in some ways, so yes it can contribute to your development.

Let's go back now, to a time of joy, passion and love in your youth. Where are you?_____

_____

_____

Who are you with? _____
_____ Describe the weather, the atmosphere (as we call it), the temperature, how you feel and perhaps what you are wearing if you can   member._

_____

_____

_____

_____

_____

_____

_____

Were you able to feel it? How did your body feel when you did? Was there a lightness to your body, did you feel tingly inside, did you laugh? _____

_____

_____

_____

How can you attribute this to everyday life? How can you add it in your daily routine? First start by beginning to create or recreate new feelings. Even if it's once a week to start. Allow yourself to FEEL. Thats' the key. To recap; The goal here is to allow yourself the freedom to feel good, happy, love and light. By using the youth imagery as a model for happiness, because there were no walls then, no hesitations, or fears in youth. We all were expressive in some way. Your job, or call to action is to remember that little self and make peace with the fact that that's the jewel point of which great actors are born. Great speakers, writers, leaders and motivators. This one is bigger than you think. So this tool is called **YOUTH**. Add it to your tool-box. And no youth was not wasted on the young, it was the youth that created our true selves. In acting, there are many references to "It's a child's game," "You must go in to come out." "Life is but a dream and everyone is playing you." "The joy of being alive is being in touch with that inner self, or inner child." It's important to honor and capture that spirit of the inner child again and find that feeling or feelings of love and allow them to be free in your heart and mind.

Morning exercise: When you wake up fresh from sleep, do a check-in with yourself and ask "how do I feel?" I want you to put the emphasis on the word "feel". This isn't about your thoughts, it's about how you feel. FEELING; An emotional state or reaction. Happiness, Sadness, Fear, Disgust, Anger, Surprise And if your answer is depressed, then it's your job to do a little self-help work here. It's your time to take the reins for your life and build yourself up here. Remember that light switch? Flip that switch now and change the way you think about yourself and your life at this moment and make it a positive. One way and it's my favorite is to do your gratitude list. Pick 5 things you are grateful for and say them out loud, or write them in your journal. Oh wait, you don't have a journal? You need our companion journal for The Process Code. You can get it here for free. www. Theprocesscode.com

It's good to journal your thoughts and growth. It's easier to see the progress.

"A personal journal is an ideal environment in which to become. It is a perfect place for you to think, feel, discover, expand, remember and dream." - Brad Wilcox

7. The Procedures

Steps in order to accomplish something. A goal, and act or action. In time the process will take hold and the procedures will become second nature as you repeat them and follow them, adding to your toolbox each and every time. By the way, a toolbox, or the toolbox of life in this reference can never have too many tools. Tools are memories and new patterns that come together to form/sculpt the new you. And, we aren't saying we are getting rid of the old you, no, it's more similar to a snake shedding its old skin and reviving the colors beneath. Your colors have always been there, you were just wearing too many layers to see it. The procedures are 3 steps that you will want to follow and practice on a daily basis.

Step one. The morning mantra (How do you feel? What's good in your life, or gratitude.)

Step two. Stand in the conviction of your goal. focus on it daily. Write it down on your calendar if you have one, put it in your phone as a daily reminder, or add it to your vision board. Don't have a vision board? What!? Oh, right, we didn't get into that part, because that usually comes later. Secret shhh. If you want to get ahead, get a whiteboard or check out my buddy Josh's company www.Writeyboards.com you can find them on Amazon as well. They are dry erase boards that come in several different shapes and sizes. Perfect for vision boards. I use a magnetic board so I can stick things to it. But if you are a visual person like me, it's beneficial to SEE your goals and progress.

Step three. Begin to own your truth, feel it wash over you and tell yourself it's okay to feel. It's okay to feel alive and allow the sunshine to shine through. Know that each day you continue this and make it a new habit, you'll become more and more comfortable. It doesn't take 7 days, or 30 days, it takes one to change everything. Because, when you make the choice to change you will see the effects of your new decision immediately around you. The choice is yours, the challenge is what you make it. I'm asking you now follow The Process Code and step into the light of a new you. A happier place of awareness and love. You want this, right? Then open that door.

BREAK TIME!

Yes, this is a chapter of relaxation and reflection. Take a break now and let your feelings pour out. You might have tension, or frustration building. It's time to acknowledge it and allow it to pour out like water from a spout. Take the pressure off yourself now and put on some soothing music, or music that calms you. No pressure, no outcome needed. No boundaries, no walls, no judgement, no hesitation. Just write it out and allow the stream of consciousness to fill the page. It can be about anything. What ever is in you now, this is your time to release. Ready? GO!_____

_____

_____

_____

_____

_____

_____

_____

_____

_____

_____

_____

_____

_____

_____

_____

_____

_____

_____

_____

_____

_____

_____

_____

_____

_____

_____

_____

_____

_____

Ahhhh…. Better? Well done!

What's working? This is also a great time to reflect on what is working. How the goodness in your life fills you. What's working in your life at this time? Please list the good things that are present now. Love, laughter, Joy, relationships, career, health, peace of mind. Now you._____

_____

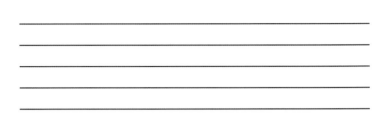

8 The Codes: Understanding the past

*"Learn from the past, live in the pres-
ent and dream of the future." - unknown*

This one is so good, I have it tattooed on my forearm. As we begin to understand our past, we unlock the memories to life in the present and as we evolve into a better understanding of self and a conviction to stand in our own truth, we can then dream of the future.

The dreaming of the future is the vision board, the laws of attraction, the awakening, but let us get back to the understanding of our past. In this case, it's your past. You are unique to your own and alone with your memories themselves, even though they mirror others and in truth, we all share similar emotional experiences. Your past, do you feel you have a better understanding of it at this time? Yes, or no? If yes, then be grateful, you have grown thus far, remember it may be baby steps until this becomes the new normal. You may want to go back and redo your questions and answers in chapter one and two. Repeat the steps that got you to this point. Breathe that in for a moment... Feel the release of the old pain and old patterns and allow that old energy to drop to the floor. Whoosh. Okay, it may not be a whoosh sound, it may be silent, but it was for effect. Just let it go. Shake it off if you need to. There you go. Again, we work very quickly as the idle mind becomes the devil's workshop and the negative thoughts begin to creep back in, so we are taking control of ourselves and creating new patterns by picking up the pace. You get it. Moving on. Oh, wait, for those of you who it didn't work for, take a moment to ask why? What isn't working? Are you not understanding the correlation between the past and the present? Or is the pain from the past still there? If you are not understanding the past, go back and redo the exercise. But, this time give yourself permission to feel the pain or anger, hesitation, angst. Listen, the past is a mess for us and I'm telling you something from personal experience. I still deal with my past as it comes up in different situations from time to time. And it affects my everyday life and relationships. But, the more and more you become aware of it's hold on you, or control over you emotionally, you will begin to shed light on it and it will no longer have an effect on you. IE: My father was loud and angry and violent, I can still hear the voice in my head and I used to avoid confrontation or loud situations because of this. I personally had to go back several times and deal with the effects of this and know it wasn't my fault, because I had guilt from a childhood of this. Once I let his control over me go, I also washed away the fear of those loud situations and found myself taking on more aggressive and masculine roles in acting as I grew. So, you may have to revisit a time or two. The other part of this is to self check yourself and ask "Am I ready?" Are you ready, or prepared to let go of the past? Oh, it never fully goes away, but the memories and the power you can pull from the past are life-altering. Imagine the freedom, of releasing something that has kept you from achieving your dreams and goals up to this point. Imagine feeling more joy, becoming more aware and awake within yourself, so that you catch yourself in the old patterns and stop it before it takes you back down that dusty old road. Imagine more peace and wellbeing. Imagine, your life and living your dreams. Yes!

10. The Codes: Shedding your skin

Picture a snake, I know I know, most people don't like snakes, but the visual of one shedding its skin is metaphorically appropriate. You notice I didn't insert an image of a snake here. :) The act of the visual is what I want you to feel. Because, when you do and you see the new you or new skin you'll be amazed by all of its beauty and wonder. The air may feel better, the sun brighter, the smells stronger, the feelings more vulnerable and the tastes will tickle your tongues. Do you think I'm joking? Go ahead walk outside with the new skin, the new you and you will see. If, and only if you allow yourself to FEEL. Feel the pleasures of your success, your richness, your depth, your wisdom, and your awareness. Remember that inner child, that little boy or girl. You must take them with you and allow them to play. That's the new skin. Challenge yourself now and get your butt out into the world and test it. Unless it's late at night and you are reading this before bedtime. Tomorrow is a new day and a great day to start with the new you. Keep your journal as to how it goes and make a note on how you feel.

Journal, Journal, Journal; Journal every day for one week, then go back and read it. You'll see where you were and where you have gone. you have it written down and some of it might sound silly, or the connection to that moment might be long gone, but there's growth even in that. Give yourself credit for the growth now. You may not see its effects fully or maybe are not as aware as you might think in recognizing the growth. Still, this is a great time to reflect and rejoice in the happiness of today! Oh, yes, I know there were days you felt like crap and that you weren't getting this. Probably in your journal or daily writing, but know the earth must be broken in order to give up life. When you plant the seed for new growth, the soil has to produce life to the seed and eventually it sprouts. Once it breaks ground, you'll notice it grows much more quickly.

Stay on track here and commend yourself for great progress. Smile, be happy at this moment, please. Ahhh, you feel that? Yes!

11. The Codes: Beginning to walk into the light

Before this all began, did you think you'd feel ready to do this so quickly? Did the chaos in your head seem more dramatic? Have you questioned your experiences throughout this book thus far? Do you feel ready to take this into your life and life's work? These are only questions you can answer for yourself, but we hope that there is less fear and a better understanding of the new you at this time. Again, if not, go back and take more time. But, if you are as courageous as we believe you are, then you are ready to walk into the light. What does this mean? Well, for some, you may see yourself walking through that door you drew or imagined in the beginning, or you may actually see yourself walking outside today, or tomorrow. Walking with your shoulders back, posture perfect, with confidence and purpose as you step out into the world.

Whatever your vision for this is, I feel you are more awake, more aware than you were before. So, regardless of your level and please do not judge yourself as there's no competition here. Your level now is greater than before. Why do I believe this? Because, I wrote this to create a spark in you, to touch something special in you. Perhaps even in the smallest way. But the seed has been planted for your growth. And it's a big deal, even if it appears small. The fact that you may laugh more at my silly writings right now then you did before. The fact that you allow more room for YOU in your life and see yourself differently. That light, that vision is the jewel point and the beginning of something even more magical. Take a deep breath, exhale and feel the air awaken your soul. Your mind becomes more active, you become more aware of your heartbeat. You are ready for the new day, new week and new experiences that await you. Take one more deep breath before you go. Okay… Now go.

12. The Codes: Questioning the Awake

Now that you are becoming more awake, you will begin to question yourself and others. As you learned, there will be more awareness to tap into more emotions. You will begin to sense others' feelings and perhaps feel and know what they are about to say before they say it. You'll begin to read body language and hand gestures, eye movement and voice patterns. Yes, you are becoming more awake, more aware and this is part of The Process Code. A good lesson to remember is the more questions you ask and realize for yourself, the more you will understand others and be able to not only stand strong around them but be more apt to adapt to their moods and emotional swings. Try this. Ask yourself what you are feeling now and why? When you see a friend or even encounter someone during your day, do a quick check-in with yourself and ask how they affected you? Did you notice what they were wearing? What color their eyes were? How they smelled? What emotion was most present in their demeanor? Did they appear comfortable, nervous, scared, emotionless, sad, angry? Were you attracted to them? Were they attracted to you? If so, how does that make you feel? The key to growth is to question your awareness daily and you'll find after a few days, weeks maybe and it will become natural. Now, you'll have to figure out how to handle each situation, but the awareness will give you the tools, yes more tools for your toolbox to better handle situations. You might find yourself getting involved to help someone who is sad or lonely by offering guidance. They may look at you, like "How did you know this?" Or "Where did you come from?" But, you will become a natural healer and helper as you grow. Please do not try and take on too much too fast as there may be a rush of emotions when you begin. It's amazing, it truly is, and I welcome you to the NEW YOU and a better way to approach the work in which you wish to live. This is your goal, isn't it? To be a better Actor, Speaker, Teacher, Coach, Parent, Leader, Presenter, Writer,

Entertainer, Artist, Entrepreneur, Student, Athlete, Salesman, Shaman? Congratulations, you've reached a new level.

Star

13. Power in Completion–The Everlasting YOU

Welcome to the last chapter in this book. For some of you, it may have seemed easy and fast. For others, this was a challenge in opening up to the self you were born to play. The real you. The truth. Welcome to your truth and the beginning of something greater. I hope you have enjoyed having me with you along the way and you have enjoyed The Process Code. We would love to hear your praise, thoughts, questions about the book and about your personal process. There's power in completion. Completion of anything is a good thing. You've just knocked out this book in a short time and we salute you. Well done. Feel that power of completion and the new you that has emerged. Oh, you may not even be aware of its effects on you yet, but you will. Give it a few days, a few weeks, things will begin to show up and reveal themselves to you. And keep your goals and vision boards in front of you, because you will begin to see changes and steps toward them. You might have already achieved a goal or two. Write new goals and visualize your dreams coming true. Seriously, this works and the power you have and the power of new growth are astonishing. The more people we can affect and share with, the more we raise the energy vibration to better ourselves and those we touch. There's no magic spell or fake meaning to this. There's no real mystery or science to figuring this out. It's a fact. The more you allow yourself to feel and understand about your past, the more you will awaken to realize the self that awaits you. The more understanding you will have of yourself and others. The more you feel, the more powerful you can become. This brings, leadership, strength, confidence, and passion. It frees you from the binds that held you in the past and helps you to realize that you are responsible for you and only you can change that. By learning the gifts of expression and feelings and emotions, you can understand the fears that once blocked you. Welcome to the new you! Yes! Yes to the greatness that has begun! The everlasting you. Yes, you may want to go back and you may stop, or run at times, but you can never turn this off. This is a new way, the new process and the new patterns that will forever be with you. Keep your dream alive.

Additional material; Making a better future for yourself and those around you. If, you are a parent or expecting parent, think again of what you have learned here and how much more aware this makes you for not only your future but the future of your little ones. As parents, we need to do check-ins with our kids and ask how they feel, what they feel and why? Get them to talk and keep them talking, because as we all know the teenage years from 14-18 are some of the toughest times in life. The more you can tap into your truth and be more emotionally stable, you'll be giving them a gift that will alter the course of their life. Remember the formidable years from birth until 4-5 years old are the most important to give them security and stability. Keep reading to them, singing to them, playing music for them and giving them a calm sound vibration so they know they are safe. What? You didn't think this entire training was only about you did you? I'll give you credit, it is mostly about you, but the bigger picture is what you do with it and how many people you can touch with the new energy and your own special skills. May it be volunteering, care-taking, coaching, writing, speaking, teaching, or simply using it in your own home. The door is open now and you can and will continue growing. I cannot wait to hear the results you all have. Even if they are rocky at first, just know if there is dis-comfort there's growth. And even if you feel numb or nothing for a while, know that feelings sometimes lay dormant as they are building. Picture fibers or strands being stretched out and the being wrapped together. It's similar to that. They may take a little more time before you feel the full effect of them, but trust they are there when you need them. Picture that door remaining open and the sunlight coming in daily. Each and every day YOU are becoming a more connected, more aware, more awake, more passionate, more expressive you.

Disconnecting; Here's an extra BONUS. A faster track to healing and growing during this time and I didn't mention it much in the beginning because I believe you will automatically just do it, but in case you are addicted to your phone, or the television as so many people are in society today, I'm going to ask you to look at that as an old pattern. How far has that pattern gotten you? Are you the type that wakes up and looks at your phone, or checks emails before you've had a moment to ground yourself? Yep, I've done it too. How does that make you feel when you see a negative email, or not get an unexpected message from someone? Kinda messes up your morning, doesn't it? Yes, it takes the pleasure out of your morning and now you gotta pull yourself together and get ready for work, or get the kids ready for school, whatever your daily routine is. That's an old pattern and not a productive one. Even with today's media-driven society and social networks abound, we MUST stop and allow ourselves pleasure time, snuggle time, stretch time in the morning. Give yourself at least 5 minutes to lay there and visualize productive thoughts, ideas, and visions of what makes you happy. Maybe it is taking the kids to the lake this weekend and seeing yourself on a canoe or a boat, or fishing from the shore. Breathing in the fresh air as you walk out onto the deck with a warm coffee or tea. Feel the beauty of things. Maybe you are excited to meet someone this coming weekend and you've set up a date and time. Allow that pleasure to wash over you. Or, simply just lie peacefully and listen to your breath. See your door and the sunlight coming in. Feel the rhythm of your heartbeat. If you share your bed with your mate, or someone close to you, hold them. Don't talk, just allow the comfort of another to recharge your battery. Okay, now you are ready to get up and begin the day.

TV is another way to avoid your own thoughts. If you are one to click it on as background noise or out of habit to fill the room with something other than silence, try music instead. Remember what you think about, or in this case, listen to, you attract. If you have the news on, you are listening to negative situations, death, murder, rape, car chases, escaped prisoners, shootings, political scandals, and fear-based programming. Because the last time I heard the news on TV is wasn't good. By the way, I do not watch television. I haven't watched the news in over 15 years, nor do I tune into any negative shows to fill the room. I choose music or silence. I like to hear nature and the birds, the wind. Okay, you might say, well Mr. Carmichael how do you keep up with what's happening in the world? I don't. If its true newsworthy, I'll hear about it. But, the filler news that is the majority to me isn't something that motivates me, nor does it inspire me to want to better myself. And I can tell you from experience, I grew up in a household of news 24/7 and it was dreadful. Unless you are a news anchor, or in the business, this won't help you get closer to you. When I stopped watching television all together I realized how much I was missing in my life. And I began going outside more, into nature and doing more productive things. The news of goings-on of America had no effect on my life anymore because I was doing what I wanted. Oh, I'm listening to calm music all the time when I write this. It's a good way to read along too. I have the music on my computer down low enough it doesn't interrupt. Make choices that better your life. Recognize those old patterns that hold you back or keep you in one place. There's not as much growth when you're lying stagnant. Remember, I am here to help and I and/or my team will hopefully be able to answer your questions and keep you on track as you go. I suggest coming to one of our live seminars or workshops so I get a chance to meet you and perhaps answer your questions in person. I look forward to doing more together. Disconnect. Breathe. Allow time for you. I'll see you soon.

Overview; Congratulations, you've gotten to the end of this book. Let's go over a few key things to see how you are doing, what you are doing with them, what you've taken with you.

Have you connected to the person from your past who has been affecting you?
- Did you do the work to release them and/or stand up to them to gain back your power? If not now, when?
- How has this changed your emotions, moods, focus?
- Have you realized your passion? What is it? Has your life begun to change in order to achieve your goal?
- Are you going in the right direction?
- What's holding you back?
- Have you noticed what your friends and peers are saying, doing? Are they reacting differently?
- How is your personal life? Is your relationship better? Are you asking for what you want?

- Have you set a money goal?
- What are the most profound things or moments that have happened to you since you started this book?

Join me. Please follow The Process code on Youtube and @therealjoshcarmichael on Instagram to keep up with our schedule. Join me for private sessions, or group meetings. for bookings please contact:

Additional material; Making a better future for yourself and those around you. If, you are a parent or expecting parent, think again of what you have learned here and how much more aware this makes you for not only your future but the future of the little ones. As parents, we need to do check-ins with our kids and ask how they feel, what they feel and why? Get them to talk and keep them talking, because as we all know the teenager years from 14-18 are some of the toughest times in life. The more you can tap into your truth and be more emotionally stable, you'll be giving them a gift that will alter the course of their life. Remember the formidable years from birth until 4-5 years old are the most important to give them security and stability. keep reading to them, singing to them, playing music for them and giving them a calm sound vibration so they know they are safe. What? You didn't think this entire training was only about you did you? I'll give you credit, it is mostly about you, but the bigger picture is what you do with it and how many people you can touch with the new energy and your special skills. May it be volunteering, caretaking, coaching, writing, speaking, teaching, or simply using it in your own home. The door is open now and you can and will continue growing. I cannot wait to hear the results you all have. Even if they are rocky at first, just know if there is dis-comfort there's growth. And even if you feel numb or nothing for a while, know that feelings sometimes lay dormant as they are building. Picture fibers or strands being stretched out and the being wrapped together. It's similar to that. They may take a little more time before you feel the full effect of them, but trust they are there when you need them. Picture that door remaining open and the sunlight coming in daily. Every day YOU are becoming a more connected, more aware, more awake, more passionate, more expressive you.

keep your dream alive
"Think Big from the Heart, not the Ego." - **Anonymous**

BONUS - EGO

The Empty Chairs: You see the empty chairs above right? They remind me of my thoughts. One is, perhaps scattered and not clear, or hasn't come into focus yet. The other may be dark and angry or fearful and the other may be dreamy and loving. For me, this is the ego and I as I explained this recently, it's as if there are several characters in play when it comes to ego. Two mainly that act as plus or minus, positive/negative. In a story i have told, or tell often I laugh as I recall the image of me in my youth dis-covering who i was and creating the man I have become today. But, it came with great cost. I literally mean great $$$$ cost. You see I was searching, so this meant creating my own style and keeping my hair tight, my look polished, my body in shape. There was a lot to take in. It was like one day i would be open and just allow the energy to flow properly, and the next I would feel insecure and have to go buy a new motorcycle and a badass t-shirt so I could show up in style. It was a lot for me to be cool. I mean i was trying to impress. Any of you feel this? Well, lets just say it changes as you become comfortable with you. As i aged and grew into myself and found success in what I was doing i just all of a sudden had a style, and i began to not care what others thought of me, so it freed up more time and growth for me and my adventures. Back to the empty chairs. What do you see? Which chair are you today? How long have you been this chair? _____

_____

_____

_____

_____

_____

_____

_____

_____

_____

_____

_____

_____

_____

_____

By choosing a chair, you are choosing to focus on the attitude or characteristic of the ego at the moment. Know, that when you feel cocky or arrogant, or insecure (and you can admit it) you will notice the mood change of the ego. The need in that particular scenario will vary. What can you do to change it, or alter it? That's simple. Acknowledge it. Make note of how you are feeling and when you give it a feeling, an emotion, you will no longer have the same desire to be what the ego was suggesting. By doing this, you can tame the mood swings and begin to silence the ego-self that strives for the wrong type of attention. Become the one who focuses your attention on what you feel and your desires of what you feel. The ego will only grow when fed with insecurities. This is a warm-up for what's to come. In The Process Code Companion, we will get into the self - esteem and the growth of self. If you are like me, this just keeps on coming. The vision, the growth, the wisdom, the ability to learn and understand. the truth, the reality.

** What your life could look like when you change the programming and vibrate at a higher frequency. Yes, this may sound corny to you, but for lack of better words, it is the best possible way to explain it. But, in case you didn't like that verbiage, here are some suggestions to think about and change in your daily life.

"Everything in life is Vibration." - **Albert Einstein**

keep your dream alive

11 Things to raise your vibration in everyday life.

1. Stop watching the news and negative stories. Oh, I bet that's tough on for a lot of you. This is number one because it's probably the most common thing we all share if you share daily with others. I haven't watched the news or TV for that matter in over 15 years. The news was never one of my things. But, you can't avoid it. I walk past it at the gym, and everyone on the stair masters is glued to it. The majority of us are programmed to desire more negative. So STOP!

Become the minority and the awake!

2. Change your music choices, or at least try a new pandora or Spotify channel with more Uplifting music.

3. More Vegetables? yep, your mother told you when you were young. Did she know something we have forgotten? By eating more veggies and cleaner foods it's proven you can raise your energy vibration.

4. Join the gym or tennis club. Get Moving! You'll have more energy just by getting out and who do you think you'll meet at the gym or working out? People who care about their bodies more and most likely are eating healthier.

5. Breathing exercises. Yes, breathing or learning to breathe right, allows more blood flow and more oxygen and will raise your attention span as well as your heart rate, causing more energy.

6. Try going to a comedy or reading/watching something funny. Laughter increases endorphins.

7. Get out into Nature. You've heard me talk about this one. I love nature, the beach, the mountains, even just sitting in a park on the grass. Magical.

8. Hey! Love yourself dammit!

9. Try a new group of friends or go to new places to meet more enlightened people. Join meet up or our online group

to find these people. Let's become the majority.

10. Clean out the closet. Have a garage sale, clean the closet. Throw out old stuff, which is old energy and allow room for the new.

11. Allow yourself to be open to new things and new energies. Okay josh, how do I do that? I get it, I say a lot of things in here from years of experience and I don't expect all of you to get everything or make the gigantic leaps without a safety net. Wait a minute, yes I do. LOL. Seriously though, this is YOUR time!. It's all about you and your growth and I know you will have doubts, setbacks, resistance, and fears. That's all normal. But, that's why you've chosen me and this work. I want to help each and everyone one of you along the way. it doesn't come from a book or a single page. It comes from training, live-action. Some of you can are willing to do this by yourself. Others, if you are like me, need guidance and the inspiration to look someone in the face and hear their passion and challenges right in front of you. If you are like me, you want to be pushed and questioned in your actions to make the most of this work and to make it happen a lot faster! That's me and I'm offering this to you. When you finish this book and you do the work in the Companion book, you'll have more tools. The next step is to put them into action. That action sometimes requires getting a coach or a mentor, someone to help you. So, again, I'm here for you. In the meantime, keep going and here are a few things to try in your diet.

Springwater or water with High Alkaline 9.5 pH. water. I met a man who cured himself of cancer by drinking high alkaline water. He suggested 8.0 pH or higher. I drink it daily.

Herbal Teas

Honey for sweetener

Raw Chocolate /Dark chocolate

Fresh Fruits

Seeds/Nuts (Raw)

Fresh veggies (Raw)

ABOUT THE AUTHOR

J osh Carmichael is an Award-Winning Actor, Writer, TV Host and coach, who travels frequently speaking and coaching to groups around the country. He can often be seen on TV commercials nationally and weekly online the hit show "I'm So Vain." You can find it on Facebook and Youtube. As an actor, he has starred in over 180 national TV commercials and has been coaching since 2004. Mr. Carmichael grew up on a farm in Kansas far away from everything. "I was a young man in the middle of wheat field plowing up last year's harvest while sucking up a lot of dust and hot sun. If you are not familiar with the plains of southwestern Kansas, it is perhaps one of the windiest areas in the United States. Like a snowstorm in the middle of winter, the summers are as brutal as the horrific dust bowls. There I was, a fourteen-year-old boy dreamer and a young man already questioning life and my surroundings. But on this particular day, I began a different kind of dream. I began to dream outside of the walls that were once my borders.

As I stared at the emptiness ahead, there was a calm understanding that I was meant to do more". Thus the inspiration behind The Process Code.

That dream would begin to manifest at 21 years old when he was discovered in a dance club by Ford models in NYC. Josh's journey led him to Hollywood in 1990 where his dreams became reality. As a published poet his writings would not see the printing press until much later in life. Now, with The Process Code, Mr. Carmichael is able to help others who may have similar beginnings. This book and course work are used to motivate and inspire those who have a dream around the globe. The Process Code is something dear to us, we hope it has inspired you. Thank you.

THE END

THE PROCESS CODE

Unlocking your past to live your future

Josh Carmichael

The process code is changing peoples lives. What holds most of us back from achieving our dreams? Fear. The Process Code gives you the tools to confront that fear and understand it. Unlock your past and live your future.

Made in the
USA
Columbia, SC